True Prayers
BEAR YOUR CROSS

by Lacey Whittaker

Edited by Lil Barcaski

Published by: GWN Publishing

www.GWNPublishing.com

Cover Design: Kristina Conatser Captured by KC Design

ISBN: 979-8-9863922-0-2

DEDICATION

I am dedicating this book to anyone out there that chooses to count the cost. That is willing to bear your cross and say Yes to Jesus.

ABOUT THE BOOK

In this book, you will find 100 True Prayers. This is a continuation of True Prayers 1, True Prayers 2: Hear Him Speak, and True Prayers 3: Follow and Obey. Just diving in deeper and deeper. Are you willing to bear your cross and follow Him no matter the costs?

In this book there are some hard truths, battles and trials we have gone through by saying Yes.

Give up your life, follow Him. Give up the comfort and see again. Give up self and gain a best friend. Give up and choose to live. Give up, it seems so hard to do, but when you give up and really choose, you will give up to serve and honor truth.

2

No matter what, I want to be a Christ follower. No matter what, I will choose the road less traveled. No matter what, I will always say yes. Even when it takes all I have. No matter what, I will love You. No matter what, until my last breath. No matter what.

> *"And you became followers of my example and the Lord's when you received the word with the joy of the Holy Spirit, even though it resulted in tremendous trials and persecution."*

–1 Thessalonians 1:6 *TPT*

Will you make a stand for truth when your friends are sitting on the bench of right and wrong? Will you make a stand and walk on? Will you leave them behind and out from the lies and sins they choose to live in? Will you make a stand to follow Christ when everyone else chooses a different life? Choose to stand in faith. Choose today.

4

Narrow way. Narrow gate. Keep me on the narrow path. Narrow is the way. Narrow is the way. Narrow is the way. I will walk by faith. Narrow is the way. I will keep my eyes on You. Narrow is the way. I will read all of Your truth; narrow is the way. I choose You. Narrow is the way.

> *"Enter by the narrow gate; for wide is the gate and broad is the way that leads to destruction, and there are many who go in by it."*
>
> –Matthew 7:13 *NKJV*

Do you abide? Do you remain when the going gets tough? Do you remain in the vine? Do you remain? Are you willing to bend but stay in the vine? Where does your heart lie? Does it teeter between good and evil, wanting to step outside the will of God? Stay focused on truth and what He is calling you to do. Stay close to Him. Remain and abide, let Him guide.

6

I will never have to be afraid in this life I choose. This life I chose to follow You. To obey You with hard truths. To do what You say and what is asked of me. No never, shall I walk afraid or lonely. Never shall I be afraid or insecure. You are my rock and I know I will hear so clear. That still small voice I trust. Lead me and I will follow You all of my days.

"Whenever I am afraid, I will trust in You."

−Psalms 56:3 *NKJV*

Are you willing to suffer? Are you willing to suffer? Persecution? Mockery? Deep painful suffering, to walk in His will? Are you willing, to suffer for the good? For His plan? Are you willing? Called and chosen ones you will suffer, saying yes.

8

I am Your servant. I want to hear You. I want to do Your will. Tell me. Show me. Trust me to follow through. I am Your servant. I am devoted to You.

> *"Establish Your word to Your servant, Who is devoted to fearing You."*
>
> –Psalms 119:38 *NKJV*

Saying yes Lord, when I want to say no. Putting down my will, my thoughts, my ways, my habits and choosing Yours. Walking with You, eyes on Your truth. This I shall choose.

10

I'm devoted. I'm secure. I long for more. Because I sit. Because I hear. I would never trade or look back. As now, I have the greatest of all. To sit and sit alone.

> *"There's a private place reserved for the devoted lovers of Yahweh, where they sit near Him and receive the revelation-secrets of His promises."*
>
> –Psalms 25:14 *TPT*

Beatings, hits, kicks, spins, sucker punches and broken wrists, all the price you may pay, by calling on His name. Trouble will come, but it can't stay, look up, walk with Him, look up, grin and win. Look up, the cross He bore, took on so many sins and yours forevermore. You shall conquer and win.

12

Guard my heart and mind Jesus. Guard them. I pray that wrap around protection. I plead. I ask of this. Guard them, as I never want to have evil come in slowly. It leads to death. Guard them. It's my heartfelt request.

> *"and the peace of God, which surpasses all understanding, will guard your hearts and minds through Christ Jesus."*
>
> –Philippians 4:7 *NKJV*

Mocked, screamed at, lied about, and thrown in the dirt. Yeah, all that really hurts. Focus on the cost at hand, focus on your Fathers plan, He was dealt all this shade too. He was dealt and still glorified truth. He was dealt, oh how He was dealt. Learn a thing or two, drop what comes against and choose not to lose.

14

Each morning I shall look to You. I shall call upon You. I shall praise and honor You. Each morning I shall choose to trust You. Each morning as I rise, I shall worship You. Each morning I am abundantly blessed by You.

> *"Cause me to hear Your lovingkindness in the morning, For in You do I trust; Cause me to know the way in which I should walk, For I lift up my soul to You."*
>
> –Psalms 143:8 *NKJV*

W hat do you do when you hear the Savior say, what will you choose, how will you respond, will you admit when you go wrong? How will you choose, how will you let go when you know they are wrong, but your Father says go be strong. Forgive, speak kindly and see that all shall be forgiven, when you choose to follow Me.

16

I believe separation shall never come between You and me, Jesus. Oh, how I believe it will never come. No other love. This love You hold. Never shall You separate and grow cold. That's my hope.

"nor height nor depth, nor any other created thing, shall be able to separate us from the love of God which is in Christ Jesus our Lord."

–Romans 8:39 *NKJV*

Bear His cross. Bear His cross. Take His pain, never feel lost, never be ashamed. Bear His cross, go now, obey. Bear His cross and live life a whole new way. Bear His cross, say you will today. Bear His cross and die to self, Christ is gain.

18

Grant us the peace we need to walk the narrow path. Grant us the strength we need to never feel alone. Grant us this Lord, only could we ever be okay, if You granted us this peace to stay.

"Now the God of peace be with you all. Amen."
–Romans 15:33 *NKJV*

I love you Papa Stan.

I never wanted to let you go. I never wanted to say goodbye. I sit here tonight and want to cry. You were wise, you were comfort, you were support and the day you left, threw me off course. I miss your laugh, I miss your hugs, but what I miss most was your love. You didn't have to love me like your own, you didn't have to take me in and give us a home. You did. You were a father, a friend, a boss, the man. I don't want to let you go, but it's time. I will let you go and be fine. Only if I let you go and choose a new way, a new way, where you will never leave but always stay.

20

Counting the cost hurts. But You hurt too. I know I can endure. You endured more. Yes, You endured way more loss and betrayal. I can endure because You endured first.

> *"You can expect betrayal even by your parents,*
> *your brothers, your relatives and friends—and yes,*
> *some of you will die as martyrs."*
>
> –Luke 21:16 *TPT*

Let go of what you were dealt. Let go of what you felt. Let go of the why and should have been. Let go of the guilt and misses. Let go of the hurt and pain. Let go of the trial that never stopped screaming your name. Let go of the ones that left. Let go of them, that kept kicking, cutting, and tearing you down. Let go, I hear our Father say. Let go, I have come. Let go child I know your real name.

22

Your name be forever glorified. I am only a servant of Your will. I am only doing this in Your strength. I am only doing what You have called me to do, by the power of the Holy Spirit alone. Forever Your name be glorified above any other name.

> *"God, glorify Your name! Yes, Your name alone be glorified, not ours. For You are the one who loves us passionately, and You are faithful and true."*
>
> **–Psalms 115:1** *TPT*

Give up. Give in. You hear him creeping in. You hear those whispers taking you into that pit. Give up. Give in. You will never win. He tears us down and takes no for an answer. He comes back again with lies to give. He takes us down and never, never, never leaves. He slithers to the end like a dead, dead tree, until he sucks the life out of us. I will not quit. He hates us and, until we get this, we will never know how to fight and win. We will never know the battle within. The war raging inside, cast him down, cast him out. Take authority. Satan, flee. Live again, Lord, help us see.

24

Your ways higher than ours. Your plans are greater. Your plans win over mine. Always and forever. Your plans Lord. I will follow Your plans.

"Yes, Father, You've chosen this gracious plan to extend Your kingdom."

–Matthew 11:26 *TPT*

25

Moving on. Moving forward. Moving on. Moving forward. It's time to move on and leave the others behind. Leave them behind. Leave them behind. Goodbye, sorry you missed. Goodbye, I say all of this was worth the price we paid to one day be living only for His glory.

26

Be intent. Be sure. Yes or no. No need to linger in waiting or disobedience. Yes or no will do. Live this way. Be sure. Be confident.

> *"A simple 'Yes' or 'No' will suffice. Anything beyond this, springs from a deceiver."*
> –Matthew 5:37 *TPT*

Bye. Bye. Bye. Bye. Bye all that never came. Bye. Bye, it's time to fly. Away, bye, bye. We are leaving soon. Bye. Bye, sorry we missed you. Bye, bye, we have gone away. Bye, bye, we are taken. Pray, pray, pray, praying is what we do. Bye, bye, I'm sorry for you.

28

Lord, I know You will bless me. I know You want to bless me. I know You love to bless me. Blessing me is Your nature. Your kindness as a loving Father. I know blessings come from Your hand. I thank You for blessing me for all that I have.

> *"Yes! He will bless his devoted lovers who bow*
> *before Him, no matter who they are."*
>
> —Psalms 115:13 *TPT*

Gone. Left and gone, gone, gone, gone. Where did you go? Where did you hide? Gone away in disguise. Gone like a freight train. Packing away. Gone, oh, gone for good. Now I can stay.

30

I believe these mighty miracles are seen when we bear this cross You asked of me.

> "Yes, He did mighty miracles and we are
> overjoyed!"

–Psalms 126:3 *TPT*

I'm sorry you never came. I'm sorry you chose a different way. I'm sorry, it's true. I'm sorry, the torment and torture follows you. I'm sorry, it's time to part ways. My spirit is willing and my heart will obey. I'm sorry, it had to be this way. I'm sorry you couldn't come and stay.

32

Help me to love as 1 Corinthians 13:4 reads. Help me to love so gently and be kind to all. Help me, Lord, help me to love all.

"Love is large and incredibly patient. Love is gentle and consistently kind to all. It refuses to be jealous when blessing comes to someone else. Love does not brag about one's achievements nor inflate its own importance."

–1 Corinthians 13:4 *TPT*

Goodbye is never easy, but worth it. I hear Him say goodbye is the end, but a beginning of a new day. Goodbye, my heart, mind, and soul, say goodbye. I will see you again one day.

34

I shall forever walk in hearing these mysteries. I shall forever see You as my King. As I know the cost was counted and I said yes! I will be blessed to hear Your heart given.

> "And He said, "To you it has been given to know the mysteries of the kingdom of God, but to the rest it is given in parables, that 'Seeing they may not see, And hearing they may not understand.'"
>
> –Luke 8:10 *NKJV*

Shade, lies, misconceptions. Talk, chatter, gossip at your name. When does it stop? When does it rain down and pour out? I'm so sick of the hate and bad names. When will they stop talking about me? About my family? How long will it take, Lord? How long? Days, months, years, why, oh, why, oh Lord help me repent. Help me forgive all this persecution I see. Help me leave it at Your feet, to let go and move on. Let go and be strong. These hits, punches, and kicks, help me do good and not fight with them. Help me, my flesh is weak. Help me, my flesh wants to speak. Help me seek You instead. Help me rest and lay this to bed.

36

Never let me be the passive one. The one that never truly breaks free and overcomes. Never let passive enter into my heart. Never let it even start. Break that passive nature that comes over me. Break it. I ask you to leave.

> "One word of correction breaks open a teachable
> heart, but a fool can be corrected a hundred times
> and still not know what hit him."

–Proverbs 17:10 *TPT*

Help me. Cast down my opinions. Cast down my ways. Cast them down today. Cast the arrogance I brave. Cast it down today. I want to be teachable. I want to be taught. I want wisdom and everything that was bought.

> "A fool is in love with his own opinion, but wisdom means being teachable."
>
> –Proverbs 12:15 *TPT*

38

Fire. Fire. Fire and lies. Oh, how they love to crucify. They come against and knock down the fence. The wall was built, they leave with no guilt. Help me let go. Help me love again. Help me to trust and believe. This isn't all men, where do I go run and hide, when all my thoughts and wills collide? I know what You say, I know what You do. I know the truth, but dang it's hard to lose. It's hard to lose in this world. It's hard to not say a word. If that's what You are asking me to do, I will smile and be like You.

Oh, to be wise. To be wise not in my own eyes. To be wise like You. To be wise and share truth. To be wise I ask of You. To be wise is living for You.

"But the wisdom from above is always pure, filled with peace, considerate and teachable. It is filled with love and never displays prejudice or hypocrisy in any form"

–James (Jacob) 3:17 *TPT*

40

I give up. I'm done. I give up. You won. The old dirty way to fight, I no longer delight in your ways. I have learned a new way. Forgive and not take, not take another swing. Forgive and just be. Father help rescue me. I'm trying to live for only You, my King.

I want that reverential fear of the Lord. I want that fear of the Lord every day. I never want to walk away or stray. I want to stay in that fear of the Lord. As I know this brings me wisdom and not foolishness to live.

"The fear of the Lord is the beginning of knowledge, But fools despise wisdom and instruction."

–Proverbs 1:7 *NKJV*

42

Shoot them down. Call them out. Stop them from tearing us down. Kill them Lord, their ugly flesh. Hit them. Take them until there's nothing left. Fight for me. I will be still. Fight for me, I will, I will. Fight for me. I'm asking You. Fight for me, show them truth.

Trust without distraction, I ask. It's really easy to start out in His will and then a thought of disbelief comes in. A road block. A distraction. A stop sign. A dead end. A distraction. Help me look past and trust Your plan.

> "You won't need to take anything with you—trust in God alone. And don't get distracted from my purpose by anyone you might meet along the way."
>
> –Luke 10:4 *TPT*

44

When does it stop? When does it end? When will all of this be done? The end I ask, I ask, I ask and don't see. All I see is more coming for me. More hate and insecurities. What did I do, to make you hate and disagree? I loved, I tried, but you had another will, another lie. Take them Father, shake them down, take them, don't let them win this round. Stand up. Show them truth. Stand up as I honor You.

> *"Travel light, and don't even pack an extra change of clothes in your backpack. Trust God for everything, because the one who works for Him deserves to be provided for."*
>
> –Matthew 10:10 *TPT*

I want trust like this. I want belief without wavering. I want full trust in our God. Oh, this I ask. Trust. Lord, help me trust You with everything I have.

46

Mocking, boasting, fake, lies, and playing games. When does this end? Why do You forsake? For a time as this. You let this go on and on, You don't stop it. It just keeps coming and hitting and coming again. When, oh when, will I win? Attacks, persecution, gossip, and despair is all around me. It's everywhere. Help me out and look up to see. Help me, oh Lord, help me to be safe and secure. When my enemies roar, help me cast them into this cold world. Help me up, stop them from coming again. Lord, I truly repent. Help me, help me, help me win.

We are called and He will equip us to prophesy. This is a very special gift. Ask and receive. Share this gift. Share it. Share it. A gift to encourage, build up and correct. A gift that never leaves you empty or in worry or doubt. A gift given. Oh, how I love this gift to prophesy.

"And to you I prophesy, my little son, you will be known as the prophet of the Most High. You will be a forerunner, going before the face of Lord Yahweh, to prepare hearts to embrace his ways."

–Luke 1:76 *TPT*

48

Do you feel deep? Do you feel weak? Do you feel hurt? Do you feel pain with no gain? Do you feel relief? Do you feel at your peak? Do you truly deeply feel? Do you really, really feel? Do you? Do you really feel? Really, really feel? Do you feel with your whole being? Do you feel? Do you really feel? Do you feel deep? Deep, deep? Do you feel deep? Do you weep? Do you really, really feel? It's ok to feel. Jesus felt too. Let go and just be you.

Teach wisdom. Train them up. Teach Jesus. Teach them now. Teach love. Teach grace. Teach them to praise His name. Oh, teach them before it's too late. Teach them today.

> *"The rod and reproof (godly instruction) give wisdom, But a child who gets his own way brings shame to his mother."*
>
> –Proverbs 29:15 *AMP*

50

Steady and ready. Hope. Walking in deliverance and peace, knowing You hold all of our dreams and our desires. Walking steady and ready. Do not falter to the left or right. Walking steady and ready. Have hope and joy, that new things are coming. A better way. A better life. A better commitment to You, our ever-loving Father. Prince of Peace, You give us life everlasting when we choose to walk and be.

May we never give up praying. May we never give up believing You will answer. May we never grow weary and be in disbelief. The miracles and healing You have given us. May we never, ever stop praying.

> *"I prayed for this child, and the Lord has granted me what I asked of him."*
>
> –1 Samuel 1:27 NIV

52

Done. Over. Done. Over. Done. Over. You have called us out. Done and over. We are not what this world is about. We look so different in what You have called us to do. Help us to see we win and they lose. When they take their hits because they don't understand, show them Lord. Protect us from their rants. Show them Lord. Show them truth. Show them all we want, is to honor You.

Help us see being humble and lowly in this world is really the greatest to be among Thee.

"Therefore, whoever humbles himself as this little child is the greatest in the kingdom of heaven."

–Matthew 18:4 *NKJV*

54

Father, some things I will never understand. How could this really be part of Your plan? Father, some things I may never understand. Give me the strength I need, Father, take my hand.

> *"The Lord protects the simple (childlike); I was brought low [humbled and discouraged], and He saved me."*
>
> —Psalms 116:6 *AMP*

Help me live simple. Help me cast out confusion and discouragement. Help me choose simple. As I know You are simple. You are not hard or complex but simple, and loving, and compassionate. Simply, Lord I ask.

56

Let go. Dust off the old. Throw it away. Take the grip from my hands. Let go, I hear Him say. Let go, let go. What are you holding on to? Let go, let go. See me through. Let go. It's tough and so hard to do. Let go, and watch me hold on to You. Take the past. Take it back. I don't want to hear or replay. I want to move away, move forward with truth. Move. Move. Move on. I'm ready. I'm ready. Take this grip. Take this grip, that feels like a rip. Take it away. Take it now. I don't want to hold on anymore. I want to bow, bow, bow, in Your will. Your way, Father. Oh, Father, please come take all this pain.

Peace, all my days. Peace came. Peace, please stay and never take this gift you gave. Peace, stay. Peace, remain. It's Your peace I long to have, please stay.

"Be faithful to guard the sweet harmony of the Holy Spirit among you in the bonds of peace,"

–Ephesians 4:3 *TPT*

58

The cross bore our pain. The cross took on sickness. The cross held death, but the wicked kept ticking. The cross went deep, those nails, that tree. The cross took it all and now we are free.

> *"Let this mind be in you which was also in Christ Jesus,"*
>
> –Philippians 2:5 *NKJV*

I pray to have the mind of Christ. I pray those thoughts that keep coming in like a thief, flee. I pray for the mind of Christ to flow in me.

60

Kicks, spins, You win God. Oh, you win. Kicks, spins, sucker punches to the chin. All come out with all this sin. All this sin, how do You see with such eyes of everlasting glory? How do You see past the dark and hurt? How do You see? Is it worth? How do You see? How do You see, God? If I could only be a fraction of Your ever-loving forgiveness and grace. A fraction, a fraction. Oh, what kind of place would we be living in, if we chose to love and not be against.

Humble. Lowly. Humble in the hate. Humble in the sickness. Humble in the persecution. Humble in the lies told. Humble in the character attacks. Humble. In due time. Your time. I trust Your time. Not mine. I trust. I will choose humble.

"Therefore, humble yourselves under the mighty hand of God, that He may exalt you in due time,"

—I Peter 5:6 *NKJV*

62

Push through. Beat the odds. You win at all costs. Push through. Let the rest go. Be you. Be you. Be you. Push through and be you. Let the rest go. Let it go. Let it go. Let it go. Let it all go. Start new. Start new. Start new. Push through. Chosen ones, push through. I'm guiding you, leading you, I have you. I have you. Push through, I say, push through and be YOU!

> *"Whoever claims to live in Him must live as Jesus did."*
>
> −1 John 2:6 NIV

Show me. Teach me. Show me how to live like You. See like You see. Hear as You hear. Love as You love. Walk as You walk. Serve as You serve. Show me. I want to live as You lived Jesus.

64

Hated. Beat. Mocked. This is what they do. Oh, Father, help us to always serve You. In the good and the bad, persecuted, and sad. Help us Father, our hearts to be glad.

I want to obey Your commands because I love You. I want to honor You Jesus because I love You. I want to bear all hard things because I love You. I want to do Your will because I love You. I want what You want because I love You Jesus. I love You.

> *"Loving me empowers you to obey my commands."*
>
> –John 14:15 *TPT*

66

Bear my cross, I hear Him say. I walked this walk, now follow my way. Bear my cross, I hear Him shout, if it was easy all would be about. Bear my cross, no longer give in. Stand up. Be free and win, win, win.

Love. Intimacy. Obedience. The fruit we bear by these three things. This fruit will show the life union with Christ our King.

> *"But the love of God will be perfected within the one who obeys God's Word. We can be sure that we've truly come to live in intimacy with God,"*
>
> −1 John 2:5 *TPT*

68

Fear, lies, tugs, and tears. Father they are everywhere. I try to look up and away from it all. Then something hits and I am no longer standing tall. Help me when I endure all of this. Help me to bear so much more. Help me, Father. Help me see I need You now, to fill me with peace.

His grace in my weakness. His grace. My weakness. His loving grace He gives. In my torment, my trial, in my weakest points of life. In the low of the low. His grace carries me through. His grace, I find in my weakness. That's where my power comes from, that's the power to push me along.

> "But He answered me, "My grace is always more than enough for you, and My power finds its full expression through your weakness." So, I will celebrate my weaknesses, for when I'm weak I sense more deeply the mighty power of Christ living in me."
>
> –2 Corinthians 12:9 *TPT*

70

When you are running thin and get a hit. When you are low and here comes another blow. When you are fighting for air and another wind gets knocked from your sails. When you feel like you can't hold on. When you feel low and unable to see. When you want to fight the world and not care. When you want to melt into a pity of pits. When you want to see but can't get past all of it. When you want to soak in hate and in despair. When you want to curse and not care. Father, you see it all. You know my heart. Help me, Father, I was Yours from the start.

We can't throw punches or use nasty words. We should not tear down man. We can't fight a spiritual battle in a fleshy way. Ask God. Ask Him to lead, to help, to show you a new way to fight. A new way to fight. The only way to fight this warfare. There's only one way. Ask Him today.

> "For though we walk in the flesh [as mortal men], we are not carrying on our [spiritual] warfare according to the flesh and using the weapons of man."
>
> −2 Corinthians 10:3 *AMP*

72

When the season, the torment, the trials and tribulations are over. You can finally breathe a deep relief. The misunderstood, how things went, the I don't know how much I have left. We gave it our all, now we say goodbye. Teach us Lord, to always die to our flesh. To live again, see our growth and know, we always win in the end. Time to let go, I feel relief. Time to let go and believe You have the best for me.

You pushed you shoved. When that wasn't good enough you came for me again. A deeper cut, a deeper pain, you kept pushing making me wonder if God would save. He did. I called on His name. He helped me.

> *"You pushed me violently, that I might fall, But the Lord helped me."*
>
> –Psalms 118:13 *NKJV*

74

Finished and done. We won. Finished and done. We say goodbye again. Many, oh many, we may never understand. The one thing I know is true, You lead, You guide us to You. If we are in Your will, we are ok, even if the world sees in a different way.

Stand firm. The devil will flee. It may take a day. It may take a year. It may take a lifetime. He will flee. Stand firm. He will flee. It is promised he will flee. Submit to God. The devil will flee.

> *"So, submit to [the authority of] God. Resist the devil [stand firm against him] and he will flee from you."*
>
> –James 4:7 *AMP*

76

If you counted all that was lost but never which was found, how would you see the final round?

Help me remember everything You took on that cross. Help me remember the cost. Help me remember when I try so hard to lose these habits and ways. Help me remember what You did that day. Help me remember You took all sin. Help me, Father, see that You conquered and won. Nothing more I can do as You did it all. It's finished. It's done.

> "Keep in mind that we who belong to Jesus
> Christ have already experienced crucifixion. For
> everything connected with our self-life was put to
> death on the cross and crucified with Messiah."
> –Galatians 5:24 *TPT*

78

What do you tolerate? Half-truth? Lukewarm? Passive sin? Do you tolerate the borderline jokes, the gossip? Do you tolerate but feel a conviction? Do you feel that nudge from the Holy Spirit saying, exit, you know better? Go, do better, repent, come to me. See truth. Walk in truth. Don't just tolerate.

> *"Your hand-to-hand combat is not with human
> beings, but with the highest principalities and
> authorities operating in rebellion under the
> heavenly realms. For they are a powerful class of
> demon-gods and evil spirits that hold this dark
> world in bondage."*
>
> –Ephesians 6:12 *TPT*

This is so hard for me to comprehend. It's so hard for me not to fight man. Not to blame man. Not to go after man. Not to judge. It's hard for me to see I am really battling evil spirits on them. It's so hard for me to see. I could forgive more easily if I truly see. Help me see.

80

All the trials. All the tragedy we may face. Lord we only need to look to Your face. Your loving grace shines down and pours through the depths of our soul. When we stop and look, we know You hold all these trials we walk through. Help us to see them through, with You by our side, with You as our guide. Your loving gracious will, only You provide. Help us see the way. Help us see the light, it's only in our Fathers eyes. Thank you, Jesus for pulling us through. We will choose to honor and glorify You in these dark and sad days, it's our hope, it's Your power that reigns. Hug your family, hug your friends, choose to forgive the offense. You never know when the last day will be. Forgive, let go, and be free.

> "Wait on the Lord; Be of good courage, And He shall strengthen your heart; Wait, I say, on the Lord!"
>
> –Psalms 27:14 *NKJV*

Wait on the Lord. Have courage. Be of good cheer. He has His timing. He has His plan. He will strengthen you in the waiting, if you choose to draw near. To walk in patience and peace. To walk and say, Lord, I shall wait.

82

Suit up. Spiritual warfare is real. It is guaranteed when you choose Jesus. Suit up. Cover yourself. Have faith. Withstand. Endure. Know how to fight this fight the right way. Ask Jesus. Pray. Suit up, in your full armor, the battle is for you and for me. We will conquer, we will win. We are equipped. Suit up.

"Therefore, take up the whole armor of God, that you may be able to withstand in the evil day, and having done all, to stand."

–Ephesians 6:13 *NKJV*

Do you battle and feel like you lost? Do you go again another day so strong? Do you fight just to lose on your knees? Do you ever think, why is this happening to me? Do you love at all cost? Do you play it safe or count the cost? Wherever you are at today, just know He is a savior that loves to shine grace.

84

Strong. Fearless. Warrior. A soldier for Jesus Christ we are. We are His soldiers armored walking and talking, teaching and loving. Soldiers we are in faith. Soldiers in this day. A Soldier for Christ the rest of our life.

"You therefore must endure hardship as a good soldier of Jesus Christ."

–II Timothy 2:3 NKJ

Modify, change, and correct. Adapt.

Adjustment, adjust. Adjusting, adjust, adjust, adjust, adjust, adjust, and trust. Trust, trust, trust, trust, adjust. Adjustment, adjustments all around. All align with the crown, the crown of life. It's adjusting to me, your King of Kings, Holy and True. It may look way different for you. It may look way different for you. Adjust, trust I have you where you ought to be. Trust, oh trust in me, in my glory, my plan. Adjust, adjust, adjust, adjust surrender it up. It will be a lot easier when you surrender it up. Surrender now, surrender now in your bow. Surrender now, now, now trust and see. Trust and be. This is all new, a new way the only way, the best way. Trust me, trust me, trust me. It may seem off or different but it's Me. I know you don't like change, but this is a good change. Go trust and believe.

86

Dying means to gain. We die and we gain. We gain Heaven one day.

> *"This is a faithful saying: For if we died with Him,*
> *We shall also live with Him."*
>
> –II Timothy 2:11 *NKJV*

> *"Consider it nothing but joy, my brothers and sisters, whenever you fall into various trials."*
>
> –James 1:2 *AMP*

Joy and trials go hand and hand. It's really hard to grasp and understand. Joy and trials produce strength. Strength for you, strength for me. Strength pulled from our loving Father. Always there, always His plan.

88

I'm a writer. I love to write. It brings me joy. It brings me might. I feel safe and closer to You. Like a dream written from You. I love to read but I love to write. You are my heart's delight. Everything I say, everything I am, Lord, You hold me in the palm of Your hand. Speak now, speak truth. Speak to your servant that loves and honors You. Speak, I'm listening. Speak Your words glisten on my ears. Oh, how I love when You speak so clear. Thank You, Lord for this gift to write. I don't know where I would be, I don't know how I would fight.

"bears all things, believes all things, hopes all things, endures all things."

—I Corinthians 13:7 *NKJV*

Bear. Believe. Hope. Endure. Repeat. Win the war. Endure.

90

Turn your cheek when you get slapped. Turn your cheek when you are in defeat. Turn your cheek when a punch is thrown. Turn your cheek when the unknown comes from out of sight. Cast down those lies. Cast down those hits. Father, help me repent. Help me turn my cheek when all these things come and hit me.

"But I tell you not to resist an evil person. But whoever slaps you on your right cheek, turn the other to him also."

–Matthew 5:39 *NKJV*

Do you do the hard things well? Do you strive or sit in bitterness and defeat? Do you do the hard things well? Do you complain or receive this as an opportunity for growth, for the unknown? Do you do hard things well or do you bust at the seams, crack in your insecurities. Do you do hard things well? You can. Ask Jesus to hold your hand, lead you through and always, always show truth.

92

"Then Jesus said to his disciples, "If you truly want to follow me, you should at once completely reject and disown your own life. And you must be willing to share my cross and experience it as your own, as you continually surrender to my ways."

–Matthew 16:24 *TPT*

What does it mean to disown your life? Die to self. Follow Him. Trust Him. Believe Him. Honor Him. When times are good. When times are tough. Follow Him. Surrender your will daily. Pick up your cross daily and follow Jesus with everything you have, no reserves, everything you are. Live like this today. Choose His way.

Are you dedicated? Are you loyal? Are you faithful? It's really easy to start in the beginning, telling the Lord you have my all and all. But as time passes, trials come. Do you fall apart and say you are done? Where does your loyalty lie at the end of a hard day? Do you choose to stay and pray? Every day, wake up and say, Lord, no matter what, You are mine and I am Yours and we will walk through this day together forever, this I will proclaim. Forever I will stay dedicated and devoted to You. Forever it's true.

94

"*I affirm, by the boasting in you which I have in Christ Jesus our Lord, I die daily.*"

–I Corinthians 15:31 *NKJV*

Die daily. Daily I die. Each day I choose to die to self.

> *"For which of you, intending to build a tower, does not sit down first and count the cost, whether he has enough to finish it—"*
>
> –Luke 14:28 *NKJV*

He has asked us to count the cost to follow Him. Is your yes, your yes until the very end? Is your yes still yes when it just got really hard? Is your yes, a yes when He says give up that old life and those friends? Is your yes, your yes when He asks you to do the unthinkable and leave that church you loved to move along? Is your yes still your yes when He asks you to leave that family member be and take up your cross and follow me? Is your yes, your yes when you go through a terrible sickness and loss? Do you say yes at any cost? Is it yes to the very end? Count the cost your yes wins.

96

Disappointed, shook, discouraged, unwell, hurt, do you ever feel these feelings of despair? Do you ever wonder if anyone truly cares? Where did they go, what did they do, how come all the sudden they aren't there for you? All these things that come and go, all those things that stopped your flow. Lord how many more times will we be disappointed, battered, bruised, unloved by these people that say they follow You? Where is the love, where is the support, where, oh where? This seems off course. We are called to be one, but everyone is one for themselves. Dying off, nowhere to be found, Lord, help me understand and be well. Help me let go and see, when disappoint comes it has to leave. Lord, help fill this empty void with praise. Never shall we be disappointed another day.

Writing is my weapon. Your words are like my breath, air breathed. I believe what You say, and say what You do.

"And take the helmet of salvation, and the sword of the Spirit, which is the Word of God."

–Ephesians 6:17 *AMP*

"The tablets were the work of God; the writing was the writing of God engraved on the tablets."

–Exodus 32:16 *AMP*

"I will keep Your law continually, Forever and ever [writing Your precepts on my heart]."

–Psalms 119:44 *AMP*

"But if you do not believe his writings, how will you believe my words?""

–John 5:47 *AMP*

"Then He stooped down again and started writing on the ground."

–John 8:8 *AMP*

"Therefore, be careful, so that the thing spoken of in the [writings of the] Prophets does not come upon you:"

–Acts 13:40 *AMP*

> *"I will wait for You, O You, his Strength; For God is my defense."*
>
> —Psalms 59:9 *NKJV*

Do you defend yourself? Your character? Your family? Your children? Your spouse? What about when the lies are thrown and said about you? Do you rear up in defense? Do you fight and scream? Do you shout and cause a scene? Oh Lord, these troubles come and my flesh wants to fight but my spirit stays in peace knowing You are my strength and delight.

99

Piercing Victory, He wins over Everything!

> *"Yahweh is King over all! Everyone trembles in awe before Him. He rules enthroned between the wings of the cherubim. So, let the earth shake and quake in wonder before Him!"*
>
> —Psalms 99:1 *TPT*

You are King and reign over heaven and earth. I fully believe in You and eternity. I believe that day on Calvary. I believe, so, I have agreed to bear my cross. I have chosen this because You chose me first.

ABOUT THE AUTHOR

I believe it's the Father, the Son, and the Holy Ghost, and everything else flows from it. I have an amazing husband, Justin, of fifteen years. I have two precious daughters that make my world go round. Addie, 14 and Liv, 9. We reside in Bourbon, MO and founded True Love Ministries. My heart is to flow from the heart of Jesus and tell the world the relationship with our Father is the most important of all.